Potentials

Investing opportunities for everyone, no matter the size of your wallet.

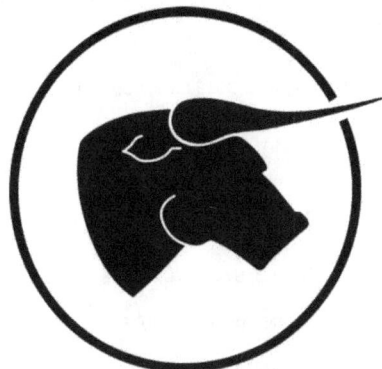

Advanced Gold Exploration Companies in the Abitibi Greenstone Belt

5 gold companies with significant grow potential in one of the largest gold area's of Quebec.

E.E.J. Convens

Gaelic Victors

ISBN-13: 978-1070777078

ISBN-10: 1070777078

D/2019/14.286/1

Independently published

Always do your own due dilligence before investing and make sure your investment suits your investor profile.

www.gaelicvictors.com

Table of contents

Preface

Investing in physical gold is a protection of purchasing power. Throughout history, gold has always proven to be a safe haven for your assets. You do not invest in physical gold to achieve a certain yield or to speculate on the volatility of the gold price. Physical gold in your portfolio will deliver an expected added value in the longer term, at least that is what it has done throughout the evolution of the monetary system. The expectations are that it will continue to do so in the future.

As a stock market investor, you can get a return on your money by finding interesting companies that generate a nice profit for your portfolio by an increasing stock price or by dividend returns. A disadvantage of companies that pay a dividend return however is that they are subject to the market movement and the accrued debt ratio of the company.

When you invest in the stock market, risk is something you will have to endure and it can never be excluded and although stock market crashes are sometimes predictable, one can never rule out the unexpected.

A black swan can land in the large equity pool at any time and cause serious storms for the listed companies. Large companies can limit their dividend payments due to an excessive debt ratio or for reason of lower profits. Recently we have even seen that there are large companies that have cut their dividends by as much as 50%. Small investors are always the victims.

Investing in commodities can be an interesting alternative, but without the necessary knowledge this will invariably lead to huge losses. The only commodities with a relative certainty of value retention are those related to mining. One such example are the phsysical metal mining companies. Influences such as weather have much less impact on a metal in the soil than it has on a crop that requires the necessary nurturing.

Physical metals have a certain value and this value can be calculated. The metal value is therefore one of the indicators to determine the value of a share of a mining company. Most analysts use the same formula, with one expection: the re-evaluation of the mined residual material. For this calculation, a widespread diversity of formulas is used, leading to large differences in the outcome. Of course there are many other indicators that help determine the value of a share. Business results, such as cash flow, EBIT and EBITDA, provide valuable information, but often—much more important than the figures—is the quality of the management team and the political situation in the country where the mine or potential mine is being built. The journey from exploration to production takes time, a lot of time. The timeframe between the search for gold (exploration) and the casting of gold (production) can easily take 10 to 14 years. It is therefore also important to be able to make an evaluation of the political situation in the long term.

Investing in metals or other commodities is considered to be speculation. I personally believe that investing in S&P 500 shares is more subject to speculation because everything depends on the ability of a management to run the company by its decisions and by political or geopolitical events. Very often, you can only take action to sell or buy their stocks after they have made a report available for their investers. By that time, most of the damage is allready done and losses are made. In recent history, we have witnessed all too often that multinationals made wrong investments and that bad decisions were made. And as always at that moment, small investors will pay the price.

With mining companies, ofcourse things can go really wrong aswell. Certainly, the former mentioned capabilities of management and the uncertain political and geo-political events play a huge role in the reliability of the value of the stock. However, I would like to point out one huge difference between a stock from a S&P 500 company and a stock from a mining company. A mining company's value is found underground, and stays there as long as it is not mined. So, nomatter what happens in terms of management, political or geopolotical events, the metals hidden underground stay where they are and keep their value.

So, in addition to physical gold, which, as stated earlier, is a safe investment to have in your portfolio, you can also invest in the companies that make it their business to get this shiny yellow metal above ground. These can be exploration, development or mining companies. The investment risk is from high to low in the same order. When a crisis arises on the financial markets, institutional investors (bank funds, insurance funds and other similar funds) often seek their salvation by fleeing to physical gold. As a result of this run on physical gold, forms of investments in paper gold (ETFs, bonds, futures and more) come under pressure as they can no longer be converted into physical gold because of the lack thereof. You see, much more paper gold has been and still is traded than there is physical gold in the world. This is the risk of paper gold one should certainly be aware of.

Investing in mining companies can therefore be a solid alternative because the metal, in this case gold, is indeed present in the soil as a reserve. The confirmed reserves mentioned in the feasibility study can be found in the ground and can also be mined in the future. Investing in gold mining companies can therefore be a huge hedge when you are building up your portfolio. On the other hand, because speculation is mentioned, there is also the possibility of losing your entire investment, so you should always due your own due dilligence thoroughly before making any investment decisions.

The last 10 years, little attention has been given to gold, with the small exception of the short gold rally that occured in 2016. Alternative investments, such as crypto coins or cannabis, are the flavour of the day and the place to seek new fortune for many investors. One should keep in mind however, that in an inevitable subsequent all-destructive financial crisis, it might become clear (again) that crypto currencies and cannabis cannot offer any resistance. The ensuing consequence might very well be that—once again—gold and gold mining companies will create spectacular gains for their investors.

I wonder if one might be able to compair the love affair between crypto currencies and their investors to the tulip madness in the Netherlands in the early 17th century. The insatiable greed for tulip bulbs resulted in a mania which had a huge impact on society as everyone wanted more, bigger and better pieces of the cake. Exuberant high amounts were paid for the bulbs, solely based on the color of the flowers they would bring forth. Wealth and poverty quickly changed hands, but the final blow was handed out when the madness inevitably came to an end. In all this mayhem, those that were smart enough, held on to their gains and by becoming wealthy individuals, they transformed their lives and that of their loved ones for the better.

It is not my purpose whatsoever to talk bad about crypto coins; and only time will tell if the quoted comparison with the Dutch tulip madness served as a good example. But the lesson to learn here is that you always have to make sure that somebody else can take a profit of your selling. No matter where or what you have invested your money in, it might be crypto, mining stocks, other commodity stocks or S&P 500 stocks, nobody is ever able to find the exact moment to sell.

The market has its own life and is unpredictable. You can calculate if the time to buy is right, you can calculate what the stock is worth, but that does not mean that the calculated price will be payed when you want to sell. On the other hand, it might also be possible that a stock is way overvalued. If this is the case, the price of the stock on the stock market does not correlate and represent the actual true value of the stock. Price and value are always two different things. And in addition, they are very subject to the personal perception and interpretation of the investors involved. That is why you better sell when the guy from the grocery store gives you advice on buying a specific stock. This might very well be the very best indicator to predict the future movement of a specific stock.

The search for valuable companies

Exploration companies have the greatest upside potential. But even before they discover resources containing significant enough quantities of the desired metal (in this case gold), there are already a lot of companies that have given up or have failed. Exploration and drilling are capital-guzzling activities and many companies are faced with too low a cash flow or have problems finding financial injections.

Exploration companies can only raise money by issuing non-brokered shares. If there is insufficient funding, the company will have to draw conclusions from it and take the necessary measures. For companies in this difficult phase, it is literally pumping or drowning. Unfortunately for many of them it is drowning, even though they have made a fairly interesting discovery.

Exploration companies that have managed to get sufficient funding can continue with exploration and drilling. Drilling results can cause a project to grow further, but if favorable drilling results are not achieved, the existence of the company may still be compromised. Investing in companies that are in this and the previous phase naturally also have a high risk factor.

Fortunately, the risk can be somewhat limited here by investing in brownfield exploration.

Brownfield exploration is further exploration at places where large deposits are found already, for example at or near sites where other mining companies are developing, or maybe already producing.

Greenfield exploration on the other hand, is done on places with no previous exploration history. This also means that there is no historical data readily available for the site. Understandably there is no doubt that the latter carries the most risks.

If further exploration yields favorable results, the company will issue a preliminary economic assessment (PEA) or a National Instrument 43-110 (NI 43-101). Herein the drilling results and the metalurgical results are announced, and also what the metal recovery will-be. The PEA is important for both the company and the investor. The company can decide through the PEA whether further exploration is justified. An investor can gain more insight into the project through a PEA and on that base decide to invest or not to invest.

Although along the process of exploration, the risk lowers, it certainly does not disappear. The company will now probably be ready for new funding and will again issue new non-brokered shares to continue the financing of the project. More shares also means a lower shareprice potential. Determining the value of a company, including the resources (in this case the raw material gold) by the number of shares, will obviously give a better yield when the company has issued less shares.

When you have interest to participate in a non-brokered placement, you can contact the company directly. Some companies also accept small investors in its non-brokered placement programm.

One of the benifits that come with the non-brokered placement of shares are the warrants. These give you the option to buy new shares at a certain price (mostly the shareprice used for the brokered placement). As an invester, it is now possible to buy more shares of the company when the warrants expire.

If the share is listed higher at the expiry date of the warrant, you—as an investor—can do great business. It is also possible that the share is listed at a lower price. This leaves you with two options: you can leave the warrants for what they are, or you can opt to pay the price difference.

Insiders or the management of the company are likely to use the warrants, even if the price is higher then the listed price. They do this first and foremost because the act generates trust for the general public. Second, if the listed price (brokered shares) is not too far away from the issued warrant price, paying the difference is actually cheaper then having the warrant expired and buy brokered shares. In this case, only the difference is due.

When the company has managed further funding of the project, new drilling programmes will take place. In the event that the company can increase its resources they will—at the end of the drilling programm - issue a Pre-Feasability study. In the Pre- Feasability study, the resources are more defined and are defined as measured and indicated resources.

The results of this study is more trustworthy than that of the previous inferred resources. Thereby, it will attract more investors when the company needs further fundings. The risk at this point of investing is still present, although not as speculative as before.

A Pre-Feasability study is very important for the company. Now, management can start thinking forward and decide whether or not they want to develop the project towards building the mine. Maybe they will lean towards a joint venture or they might decide to sell the property (project).

If the company decides to go on with the project, they will work towards the Feasability study (FS) or Bancable Feasability Study (BFS). As most companies at this point are still exploration companies, they probably need new fundings. New non-brokered shares can be issued to achieve this goal. The company is now becoming a development company.

It is important to know how many shares the company has issued in relation to the position on the mining curve. In the event that the shares have been issued in numbers far too large, it may very well be that investors are withdrawing. In this case, the company will keep experiencing difficulties in financing the development.

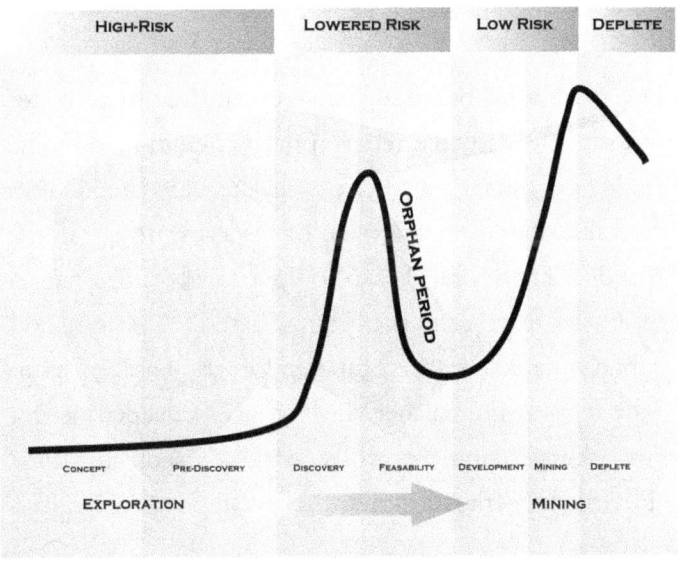

Gold related mining companies

This book will discuss a number of gold exploration and development companies which deserve the necessary attention. The book series is called "Potentials" for good reason. In it, the companies that are analysed and discussed, are expected to generate a certain added value for their investors. In other words, they are companies with potential.

The value of the gold reserves in the ground, or the value of the other minerals with a gold equivalent, reflects the potential value of a share.

The value ratio between the stock and the price is not an exact given. The effective price is determined by the market segment and this can deviate very much from the value, based on the value of reserves present in the ground. Therefore, I can only provide information about the reserves in the ground based on information publicly stated by the company. On the basis of company reports and balance sheets, I gain a deeper insight. For every company that is discussed in these "Potentials" series, a more extensive report will be available that can be ordered through our website www.blackbullassets.com and Amazon.

Disclaimer

Black Bull Assets and its staff do not give you professional, financial or investment advice. The content of these business presentations cannot be used to make investment decisions. Although every effort is made to ensure that the content is correct, we cannot guarantee the accuracy of the information or data displayed. Black Bull Assets and their staff are not responsible for your investment decisions. The information provided may not be relied upon when making specific transactions. The content only reflects the personal opinions of our staff. When investing, you must understand the inherent risks associated with stock trading and that you may lose your original investment partially or entirely. If you have doubts about an investment or a financial decision, you must seek expert independent advice. Permission is required if you wish to refer to data or information from this book. By reading this book, you agree to this disclaimer.

Monarques (Monarch) Gold Corp.

Monarques Gold Corp. is a development and small mining company with development projects as the Wasama Gold Project. The company holds a 100% interest in the Wasamac property which includes 3 mining concessions and 12 mining claims. The Wasamac project is, as the title of this Potentials book already mentioned, located in the Abitibi Gold region in Quebec (1).

A Feasability study of December 2018 tells us that the Wasamac project can produce an avarage of 142,000 Oz of gold per year over 11 years mine production (2). The project has a internal rate of return of 23.6 % pre-tax and an Net Price Value of 522 Million C$. The Pay back period is 3.6 years pre-tax (3). The project has a cash cost of 720 C$ per Oz (550 US$ per ounce) (3). The all in sustaining cost is 826 C$ per Oz (630 US$) (3). The project has a capital expenditure of 464 Million C$ including 230 Million C$ for a mill and tailings facility (3). The mine infrastructure is near the Trans Canada Highway and a railway and has an easy acces.

The Wasamac deposit is under explored at depth and along strike. This could very likely show an increasing of reserves in the near future.

The NI 43-101 technical report or the Feasability Study of the Wasamac project shows us a production of 1,556,800 Oz of gold over a life of mine with an average diluted grade of 2.56 Grams per Tonnes gold (Au) from 21.5 Million tonnes of ore (4). The average gold recovery is 88.2 % and a net smelter return (NSR) of 2.65 Billion C$ (4).

Monarques Gold Corp. has plans to start developing the mine in the second quarter of 2022 and expects to be fully operational by the end of 2022 (4).
Please note that this is important information to know how the company is situated on the mining curve.

When we make a study of the Monarques Gold Corp. projects, we can see the following:

Wasamac Project

The Feasability Study shows that the Wasamac project has 4.16 Million tonnes inferred resources at a 2.20

grams per tonnes Au (5). At a gold price of 1286 US$ per Oz, this gives a metal value of 82.05 US$ per tonnes. Total value of the inferred resources are 341,328,000 US$.

For the inferred resources, I re-calculate the value and after re-calculation the metal value is 221,863,200 US$. Please note that my percentage of re-calculation may probably differ from others and that it is my personal used percentage.

The Indicated resources are 25.87 Million tonnes at a 2.72 grams per tonnes Au grade (5). The metal value of the indicated resources is 101.44 US$ per tonnes. Total metal value of the indicated resources is 2,624,252,800 US$. After re-evaluation, the total metal value of the indicated resources is 2,099,402,240 US$.

The Measured resources are 3.99 Million tonnes at a 2.52 grams per tonnes Au grade (5). The metal value of the measured resources is 93.98 US$ per tonnes. Total metal value of the measured resources is 374,980,200 US$. After re-evaluation, the total metal value of the measured resources is 299,984,160 US$.

The Proven resources are 1.028 Million tonnes at a 2.66 grams per tonnes Au grade (5). The metal value of the proven resources is 99.20 US$ per tonnes. Total metal value of the proven resources is 101,977,600 US$.

The Probable resources are 20.4 Million tonnes at a 2.56 grams per tonnes Au grade (5). The metal value of the probable resources is 95.47 US$ per tonnes. Total metal value of the probable resources is 1,950,165,690 US$.

As the Proven and Probable resources are reserves, I accept the numbers and there is no need for a re-evaluation.

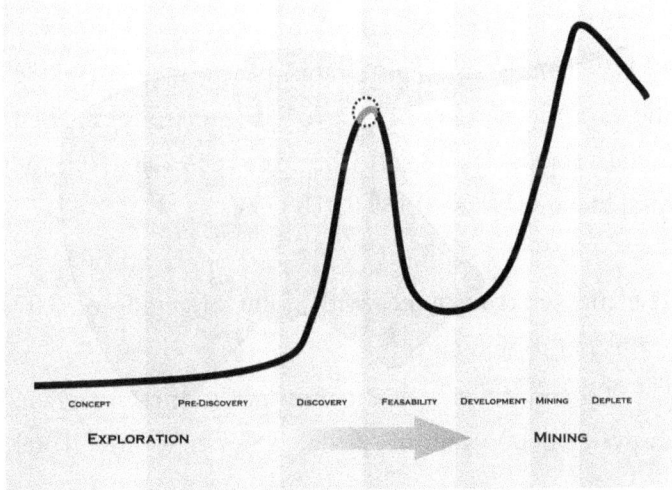

Croinor Gold Project

A next project of Monarques Gold Corp. Is the Croinor Gold project and is 100% owned by the company. The Croinor Gold project is at a Pre-Feasability stage (6).

The measured resources with a cut off grade of 5.00 grams per tonnes give:
59,000 tonnes at a 9.86 grams per tonnes Au grade shows a metal value of 367.71 US$ per tonnes. Total metal value is 21,695,411.56 US$. After re-evaluation, the total metal value is 14,102,017.51 US$.

The measured resources with a cut off grade of 4.00 grams per tonnes give:
80,100 tonnes at a 8.44 grams per tonnes Au grade shows a metal value of 314.76 US$ per tonnes. Total metal value is 25,212,276 US$. After re-evaluation, the total metal value is 20,169,820.8 US$.

The measured resources with a cut off grade of 3.00 grams per tonnes give:
111,900 tonnes at a 7.02 grams per tonnes Au grade shows a metal value of 261.80 US$ per tonnes. Total

metal value is 29,295,420 US$. After re-evaluation, the total metal value is 19,042,023 US$.

The indicated resources with a cut off grade of 5.00 grams per tonnes give:
538,000 tonnes at a 10.85 grams per tonnes Au grade shows a metal value of 404.64 US$ per tonnes. Total metal value is 217,696,320 US$. After re-evaluation, the total metal value is 174,157,056 US$.

The indicated resources with a cut off grade of 4.00 grams per tonnes give:
724,500 tonnes at a 9.20 grams per tonnes Au grade shows a metal value of 343.10 US$ per tonnes. Total metal value is 248,575,950 US$. After re-evaluation, the total metal value is 198,860,760 US$.

The indicated resources with a cut off grade of 3.00 grams per tonnes give:
997,500 tonnes at a 7.64 grams per tonnes Au grade shows a metal value of 284.93 US$ per tonnes. Total metal value is 284,217,675 US$. After re-evaluation, the total metal value is 227,374,140 US$.

The inferred resources with a cut off grade of 5.00 grams per tonnes give:

1,010 tonnes at a 9.22 grams per tonnes Au grade shows a metal value of 343.85 US$ per tonnes. Total metal value is 347,288.5 US$. After re-evaluation, the total metal value is 225,737.53 US$.

The inferred resources with a cut off grade of 4.00 grams per tonnes give:

160,800 tonnes at a 7.42 grams per tonnes Au grade shows a metal value of 276.72 US$ per tonnes. Total metal value is 44,496,576 US$. After re-evaluation, the total metal value is 28,922,774.4 US$.

The inferred resources with a cut off grade of 3.00 grams per tonnes give:

263,800 tonnes at a 5.86 grams per tonnes Au grade shows a metal value of 218.54 US$ per tonnes. Total metal value is 57,650,852 US$. After re-evaluation, the total metal value is 37,473,053.8 US$.

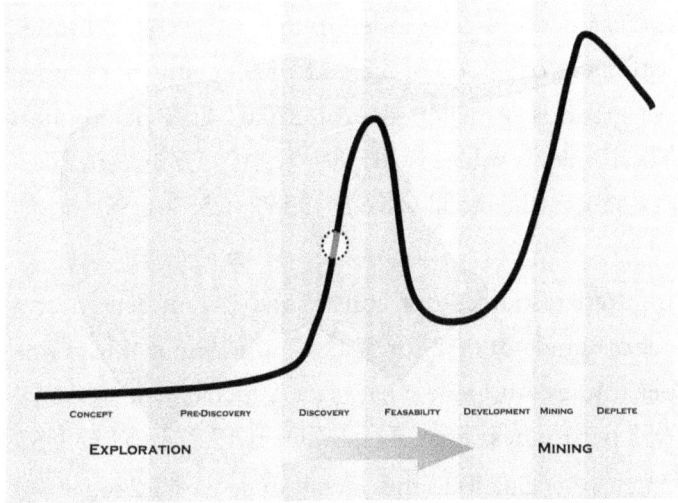

CONCEPT　　　PRE-DISCOVERY　　　DISCOVERY　　FEASABILITY　　DEVELOPMENT　MINING　　DEPLETE

EXPLORATION　　　　　　　　　　　　　　　　**MINING**

The McKenzie Break Project

The McKenzie Break Project has a resource estimate that is prepared for 2 scenario's (7).

Scenario 1:

Indicated resources (pit constrained) are 939,860 tonnes with a cut off grade of 0.52 and a 1.59 grams per tonnes Au grade. The metal value is 59.30 US$ per tonnes. Total metal value is 55,733,698 US$. After re-evaluation, the metal value is 44,586,958.4 US$.

Indicated resources (underground) are 281,739 tonnes with a cut off grade of 3.5 and a 5.90 grams per tonnes Au grade is a metal value of 220.03 US$ per tonnes. Total metal value is 61,991,032.17 US$. After re-evaluation, the metal value is 49,592,825.74 US$.

Inferred resources (pit constrained) are measured at a cut off grade of 0.52 for 304,677 tonnes at a 1.52 grams per tonnes Au grade what gives a metal value of 56.69 US$ per tonnes. Total metal value is 17,272,139.13 US$ After re-evaluation, the metal value is 11,226,890.43 US$.

Inferred resources (underground) are measured with a cut off grade of 3.5 for 318,459 tonnes at a 5.70 grams per tonnes Au grade what gives a metal value of 211.08 US$ per tonnes. Total metal value is 57,013,341.24 US$. After re-evaluation, the metal value is 37,058,671.81 US$.

Scenario 2

In scenario 2, The McKenzie Break project is shown excluded the constrained pit resources and it gives following results:

Indicated resources (underground) are with a cut off
grade of 3.5 for 422,166 tonnes at a 6.27 grams per
tonnes Au grade. This gives a metal value of 233,83
US$ per tonnes. Total metal value is 98,715,075.78
US$. After re-evaluation, the metal value is
78,972,060.62 US$.

Inferred resources are measured with a cut off grade of
3.5 for 318,459 tonnes at a 5.70 grams per tonnes Au
grade. The metal value is 212.58 US$ per tonnes. Total
metal value is 67,698,014.22 US$. After re-evaluation,
the metal value is 44,003,709.24 US$.

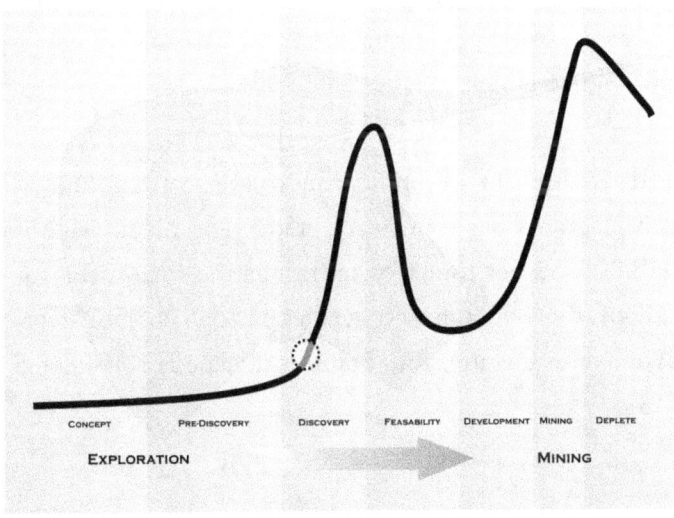

CONCEPT · PRE-DISCOVERY · DISCOVERY · FEASABILITY · DEVELOPMENT · MINING · DEPLETE

EXPLORATION · MINING

The Swanson Project

A fourth advanced project of Monarques Gold Corp. is the Swanson project in which the company has a 100% interest in the Agnico Eagle Mines property. The property owns a mineral lease and 129 claims over a total of 51.1 Km². The property is accessible year round (8).

Monarques Gold Corp. has reported following results in june 2018 (9).

Indicated resources (pit constrained) of 1,694,000 tonnes at a 1.8 grams per tonnes Au, what gives a metal value of 67.13 US$ per tonnes. The metal value is 113,718,220 US$ in total for these pit constrained resources. After re-evaluation, the metal value is 90,974,576 US$.

Indicated resources (underground) are 58,100 tonnes at a 3.17 grams per tonnes Au grade. The metal value is 118.22 US$ per tonnes what brings the total metal value of the underground resources to 6,868,582 US$. After re-evaluation, the total metal value is 5,494,865.6 US$.

Inferred resources are 17,400 tonnes at a 2.53 grams per tonnes Au grade for the pit constrained resources and show a metal value of 94.35 US$ per tonnes, or a total metal value of 1,641,690 US$. After re-evaluation, the metal value is 1,067,098.5 US$.

Inferred resources underground are 56,600 tonnes at a 3.10 grams per tonnes Au grade what is a metal value of 115.61 US$ per tonnes or a total metal value of 6,543,526 US$. After re-evaluation, the metal price is 4,253,291.9 US$.

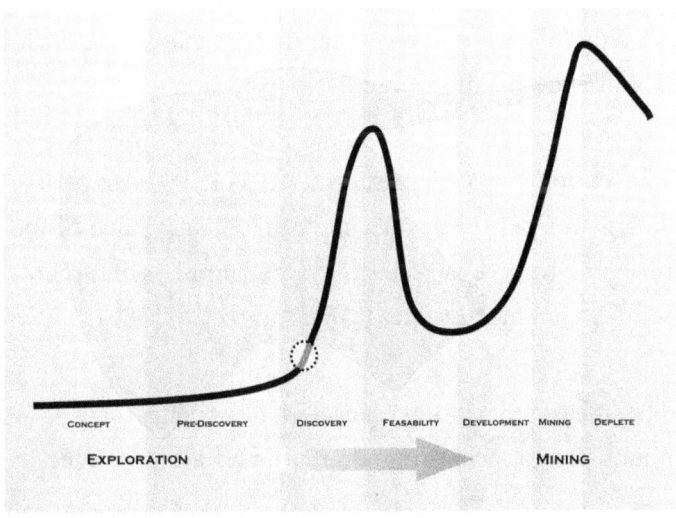

CONCEPT   PRE-DISCOVERY   DISCOVERY   FEASABILITY   DEVELOPMENT MINING   DEPLETE

EXPLORATION   MINING

Monarques Gold Corp. owns, in addition to some great projects that are in development stages, also an existing mine namely the

The Beaufor mine

The Beaufor mine (10) is an undergound goldmine with a 100% interest of Monarques Gold. In 2018, the company announced to stop its production and put the mine in care and maintenance.

The Beaufor mine has following mineral reserves:

The proven reserves are 28,100 tonnes at a 5.95 grams per tonnes Au grade. This represents a metal value of 221.90 US$ per tonnes. Total metal value is 6,235,390 US$ for the Beaufor mine.

The mines' probable reserves are 111,500 tonnes at a 7.05 grams per tonnes Au grade. The metal value of the probable reserve is 262.92 US$ per tonnes what represents a total metal value of 29,315,580 US$.

The measured resources are 74,400 tonnes at a 6.71 grams per tonnen Au grade that gives a metal value of

250.24 US\$. This brings the total measured resources at 18,617,856 US\$. After re-evaluation, the metal value is 14,894,284.8 US\$.

The indicated resources of the mine are 271,700 tonnes at a 7.93 grams per tonnes gold grade that brings the metal value at 295.74 US\$ per tonnes or a total indicated resources of 80,352,558 US\$. After re-evaluation, the metal value is 64,282,046.4 US\$.

Inferred resources are 46,100 tonnes at a 8.34 grams per tonnes Au grade what gives a metal value of 311.03 US\$ per tonnes. The general total of the inferred resources are 14,338,483 US\$. After re-evaluation the metal value is 9,320,013.95 US\$.

The Camflo and the Beacon mill

The company has two more nice assets that are the Camflo mill and the Beacon mill.

The Camflo mill has a capacity of 1,600 tonnes of rock per day which can recover an average of 98.5 % (metal recovery) (11).

The Beacon mill is fully permitted and with a capacity of 750 tonnes per day (12).

According the latest and unaudited financial statements of December 2018 and 2017, Monarques Gold has a revenue of custom milling sales and revenue of precious metal sales.

The company has 9 Million C$ at hand and according to the latest financial statements, a 1.43 quick ratio. The low level of debt indicates that Monarques Gold should have no problems to make ends meet for the rest of the year and the first quarter of next year.

Developing the Wasamac project towards mine constructions will cost a lot of dollars and therefore, I believe that the company needs extra funding for it. It will probably dilute it shares but at a responsable degree of dilution.

Looking at the metal values as yet in the ground, the share value versus the metal value is still significant. Further exploration and increasing reserves will justify new fundings for the project(s).

Besides advanced projects and mill production, Monarques Gold Corp. has 5 more exploration projects, namely the Simkar Gold project, the Regcourt Gold project, the Louvem 117 project, the Camflo NorthWest project and the Monique project.

Monarques Gold Corp. has a 100% interest in the Simkar Gold property. The property has two mining concessions and 15 claims on an area of 5 km².

The Simkar Gold project has a net smelter return (NSR) of 1.5% (14).

The Simkar Gold property

The Simkar Gold property contains measured resources of 33,570 tonnes at a 4.71 grams per tonnes Au, or a metal value of 175.65 US$ per tonnes. The general total of the measured resources is 5,896,570.50 US$. After re-evaluation, the metal value is 4,717,256.4 US$.

The indicated resources are 208,470 tonnes at a 5.66 grams per tonnes Au grade that represent a metal value of 211.08 US$ per tonnes. The total metal value is 44,003,847.6 US$. After re-calculation, the metal value is 35,203,078.08 US$.

The inferred resources are 98,320 tonnes at a 6.36

grams per tonnes Au grade. The metal value is 237.19 US\$ per tonnes what brings the total metal value at 23,320,520.8 US\$. After re-calculation, the metal value is 15,158,338.52 US\$.

When looked at the general reserves and resources, based on all given numbers, I appreciate the company on an allready discounted value at 5,793,830,021.65 US\$ (5.79 Billion US\$). Based on the metal value in the ground and the appreciated company value the share-price should have a value of 21.84 US\$. The current shareprice of 0.22 C\$ is therefore heavily undervalued and that makes Monarques Gold Corp. in my opinion a buy and hold company.

The experience of the management team indicates that they will be very capable of bringing the Wasamac project alive.

The largest shareholders are Alamos Gold, Quebec Funds, Nemaska Lithium, Rob McEwen and the Oxbridge group.

Probe Metals Inc.

In 2016, Probe Metals Inc. aquired a 100% interest from QMX Gold Corp. and their joint venture partner. With this move, they added the Bonnefond North property as an extension (along strike) to the companies New Beliveau mine. The New Beliveau mine sits around and underneath a former mine, the Beliveau mine, that has produced 170,000 ounces of gold at a 3.15 grams gold per tonnes between 1989 and 1993 (15).

The New Beliveau deposit allready had an inferred resource of 9.1 Million tonnes with a 2.63 grams gold grade in 2016. This means that the New Beliveau deposit containes 770,000 Oz gold (16).

Probe Metals Inc. Was very active in 2016. With another deal, the company signed an option and Joint Venture agreement with Alexandria Metals. By signing this deal, Probe Metals Inc, could aquire ca. 160 mining claims over 72 km² and as a result, doubled its land position (15).

Probe Metals Inc, also aquired a 100% stake from

Richmont Mines with mining claims West of the New Beliveau deposit. In December, Probe Metals Inc. announced that high grade gold was found in the East to West trending gold bearing quartz-tourmaline vein, similar to these of the Beliveau mine. Drilling results were very encouraging. Val d'Or East was allready aquired earlier that year through a business combination with Adventure Gold. With all deals closed, Probe Metals Inc. was able to expand their existing resources significantly (17).

Early 2017, Probe Metals Inc. struck an option deal with Richmont Mines and took a 60% stake in the Monique Gold property, located South East of Val d'Or East. The Monique property also contained a past producing open pit mine that yielded 55,000 Oz gold between 2013 and 2015 (16).

Probe Metals Inc, drilling campaigne in 2017 was very succesfull and more gold was found on the Beliveau Deposit. At the end of 2017, beginning of 2018, the company proved that its Val d'Or East project found even more gold and the inferred resources could be upgraded to indicated resources over four deposits. Further exploration and drilling has brought its current resources at 1.4 Million Oz. New and upcomming results in H2 2019 will increase its resources.

When we look at the four deposits that are mentioned in the companies' presentation of May 2019 (18), we can calculate the resources as followed:

The Beliveau Deposit

Indicated resources of 7,510,700 tonnes at a 2.48 grams per tonnes Au grade gives a metal value of 91.91 US$ per tonnes. This brings its total metal value at 690,308,437 US$. After re-evaluation of the metal value, the total value is 552,246,749.6 US$.

The inferred resources are 6,215,700 tonnes at a 2.66 grams per tonnes Au grade what makes the metal value of the inferred resources are 98.58 US$ per tonnes. The total metal value of the inferred resources is 612,743,706 US$. After re-evaluation of the inferred resources the metal value is 398,283,408.9 US$.

The North Deposit

Indicated resources are 837,700 tonnes at a 1.54 grams per tonnes Au grade. The metal value is 57.08 US$ per tonnes what gives a total metal value of indicated resources of 47,815,915 US$ for the North Deposit. After re-evaluation, the metal value is 38,252,732.8 US$.

The inferred resources of the North Deposit are 1,820,000 tonnes at a 1.69 grams per tonnes Au grade, representing a metal value of 62.63 US$ per tonnes. Total metal value of the North Deposit is 113,986,600 US$. After re-evaluation, the metal value is 74,091,290 US$.

The Highway Deposit

Indicated resources of the Highway deposit are 687,800 tonnes at a 1.85 grams per tonnes Au grade that brings the metal value at 68.56 US$ per tonnes. Total of the Highway deposits metal value is 47,155,568 US$. After re-evaluation, the total metal value is 37,724,454.4 US$.

Inferred resources of the deposit are 748,800 tonnes at a 1.75 grams per tonnes Au grade that gives a metal value of 64.86 US$ per tonnes. Total metal value of the

38

inferred resources are 48,567,168 US$. After re-evaluation, the total metal value is 31,568,659.2 US$

The South Deposit

The South deposit only shows inferred resources of 519,400 tonnes at a 2.97 grams per tonnes Au grade. Its metal value is 110.07 US$ per tonnes what makes a total metal value of 57,170,358 US$. After re-evaluation, the total metal value is 37,160,732.7 US$.

The combination of these four deposits is referred to as the Val d'or East project.

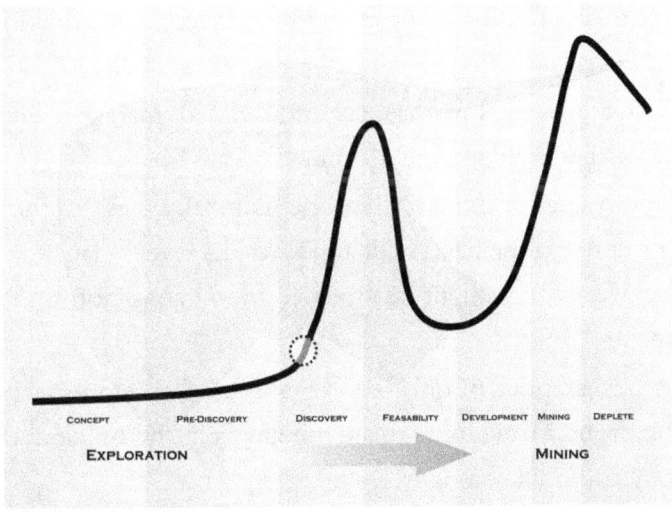

The metal value of all four deposits represents a share-price of 9.16 US$, or 12.33 C$. Shareprice is calculated, based on the fully diluted shares and according the companies' progress towards a Pre-Feasability Study and Feasability Study.

The company has a 8.39 quick ratio, based on the financial statements of the years ended december 31st, 2018 and 2017. Probe Metals Inc. is well funded for further exploration and also able to pay its bills. Whereas the debt level of the company is very low, it will probably require more funding along the way to develope the project.

When we look at the Market Cap of the company and the diluted shares, keeping its quick ratio in mind, we see a very healthy company with an exceptional growth potential.

Probe Metals Inc, has an experienced management team that is able to build a mine.

The value of metals that the company has in the ground and the healthy financial results reveal that Probe Metals Inc. might be atractive for an aquisition by a major.

At a shareprice of only 0.97 C$ and the future prospect of Probe Metals Inc., this company is in my opinion a buy and hold company.

Radisson Mining Resources Inc.

Radisson Mining Resources Inc. is one of those companies that has a long record in the business. Founded in 1983, the company has travelled a long way since, including the formation of a subsidiary company (ME) that gained the rights for exploration, extracting and selling minerals as gold and diamonds in the Central African Republic. Radisson Mining resources was active in different fields of exploration, until it decided to no longer exercise its option on MSV resources by the end of 1996. With this decision, the company gave up a 50% interest in the re-opening of the Eastmain Gold mine, 300 km Northeast of Chibougamau, Que (19). Radisson Mining Resources went on with another option of aquiring a 50% interest in the O'Brien project, which was owned by Breakwater Resources (19). The O'Brien project is located between Rouyn – Noranda and Val-d'Or, in the center of one of the most productive goldmining camps in Canada, the Cadillac Mining Camp. The O'Brien project is surrounded by 3 mines that are presently in commercial production.

With 45 million ounces of gold either in production, in reserves or in resources, the Cadillac Mining Camp ranks very high amongst the productive gold mining camps located in Canada.

In 1997, due to unfavorable market conditions, Radisson Mining Resources withdrew a 15.5 million dollar prospectus and kept a special shareholder meeting to propose a split reverse on a 4 for 1 basis (20). The companies' main purpose was to earn the option from Breakwater Resources for a 50% interest in the O'Brien property. For this, the company had to spent 3 million dollar on exploration by spring 1999. Breakwater decided to dive into the zinc business and sold all gold assets. This way Radisson Mining Resources acquired a 100% interest (21).

After a lot of drilling and exploration, Radisson Mining Resources prepared the NI 43-101 technical report for the O'Brien project in May 2018 (22). The new company presentation of May 2019 shows us its recent resources (23).

Indicated resources are 1,125,447 tonnes at a 6.45 grams per tonnes Au grade. This gives a metal value of the indicated resources of 239,05 US$ per tonnes. Total value of the indicated resources is 269,038,105.35 US$.

After re-evaluation of the resources, the metal value is 215,230,484.28 US$.

Inferred resources are 1,157,021 tonnes at a 5.22 grams per tonnes Au grade. The metal value is 193.46 US$ per tonnes. Total metal value of the inferred resources is 108,135,182.66 US$. After re-evaluation of the resources, the metal value is 70,287,868.73 US$.

According to the NI 43-101 there should be a mine life of 6 years, including 24 months of pre-production (22). Daily production is 440 tonnes with a mill recovery of 91,5%. The NI 43-101 mentions an average operating cost of 178 US$ per tonnes and an average cost of 752 US$ per Oz.

Other advantages of the O'Brien project are an easy acces to the property, a power grid that passes over the property and the project can be further explored all year round. As the project is underexplored and is open along strike and at dept, there is high potential for more discoveries to come and to increase resources towards a Pre-Feasability and a Feasabilty Study. Radisson Mining Resources is planning a resource estimate update in the second quarter of 2019.

The management team of Radisson Mining Resources has earned trust due to their life long experience. It has a strong ownership of 13% in the company, which of-course is always a good foundation to build trust with the shareholders. Also interesting to know is that the managment has only bought shares since may 2018 and has never sold these shares again. Besides the 13% hold by the managment, the companies' other big investors are Michael Gentile CFA strategy advisor, Ocim PM, US Global and Caisse de dépôt.

The O'Brien project will increase in resources when the company comes with new results. The quick ratio of 6.21 represents a healthy company without debt. To-wards the Pre-Feasability and Feasability Study, the company probably will need to acquire more funding, which they might enable through a new private offering in non-brokered shares or flow through shares.
Radisson Mining Resources has a second project that is situated in the Abitibi Greenstone Belt but no given resources can be calculated yet. The main focus of Ra-disson Mining Resources stays within the O'Brien Gold project for now.

Advanced Gold Exploration Companies in the Abitibi Greenstone Belt

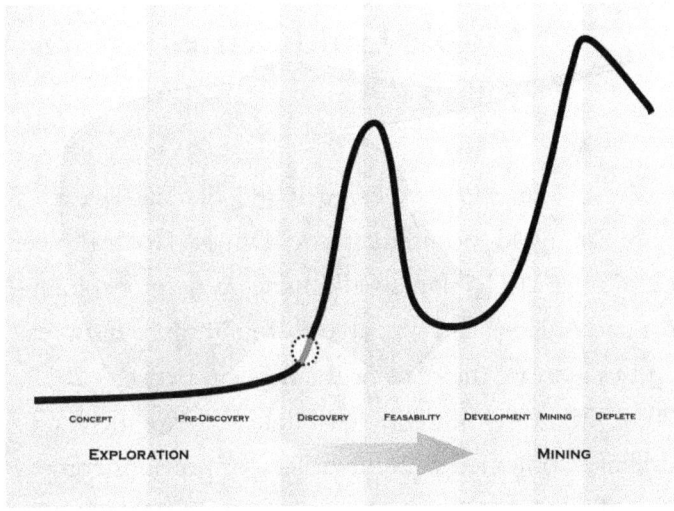

Maple Gold Mines

1976 was the year that the first discovery of gold occured at the Douay Gold Project (23). Since 2011, Maple Gold mines is doing exploration and drillings and was able to found more resources and to increase the scale of the deposit. Between 2011–2017, Maple Goldmines has done 66,000 meters of drilling. Combined with the drilling of previous companies that explored the area, a total of 221,833 meters was drilled over 757 drill holes. By the end of May 2018, the company finished their winter drilling programm and completed 21,100 meters of diamond drilling and 1500 meters of reverse circulation drilling over a total of 109 holes (24).

A private placement of 3.95 Million $ was closed at market price and no warrants where issued. The stock chart of April , when the private placement took place, shows that the market appreciated Maple Gold Mines exploration (25). Financing of the project was mainly done by insiders and Quebec Funds. This resulted in a 10% share ownership for Quebec Funds. (26).

The Technical report NI 43-101 of march 2018 (27)

shows us that the mineralized zones have the following resources:

Douay West

Indicated resources of 3,693,000 tonnes at a 2.47 grams per tonnes Au grade what gives a metal value of 91.40 US$ per tonnes. Total metal value is 337,540,200 US$. After re-evaluation the total metal value of the Douay West's indicated resources is 270,032,160 US$.

Inferred resources of 2,932,000 tonnes at a 1.39 grams per tonnes Au grade that represents a metal value of 51.44 US$ per tonnes, bringing the total metal value of inferred resources at 150,822,080 US$. After re- evalua- tion of the resources, the total metal value of the Douay West zone is 98,034,352 US$.

531 Zone

For the 531 Zone the inferred resources are 4,998,000 tonnes at a 1.33 grams per tonnes Au grade. The metal value comes at 49.22 US98,034,352 US$. per tonnes. The total metal value of the 531 Zone is 246,001,560 US$. After re-evaluation the total metal value is 159,901,014 US$.

Main Zone

The inferred resources of the Main Zone are 1,849,000 tonnes at a 1.43 grams per tonnes Au grade that brings the metal value at a price of 52.92 US$ per tonnes. The total metal value of the Main zone is 97,849,080 US$. After re-evaluation the total metal value of the Main Zone is 63,601,902 US$.

Zone 10

Zone 10 shows inferred resources of 1,864,000 tonnes at a 1.14 grams per tonnes Au grade. The metal value is 42.18 US$ per tonnes. The total metal value of Zone 10 is 78,623,520 US$. After re-evaluation the metal value of Zone 10 is 51,105,288 US$.

North West Zone

The inferred resources of the North West Zone are 828,000 tonnes at a 1.80 grams per tonnes Au grade what gives a metal value of 66.61 US$ per tonnes. Total metal value of the North West Zone is 55,153,080 US$. After re-evaluation, the metal value is 35,849,502 US$.

Zone 20

The inferred resources of Zone 20 are 1,685,000 tonnes at a 0.69 grams per tonnes Au grade that gives a metal value of 25.53 US$ per tonnes, bringing the total inferred resources of Zone 20 at 43,018,050 US$. After re-evaluation, the metal value of Zone 20 is 27,961,732 US$.

Central Zone

The last zone is the Central Zone that has inferred re-sources of 1,086,000 tonnes at a 0.96 grams per tonnes Au grade and is a metal value of 35.52 US$ per tonnes. This brings the total metal value of the Central Zone at 38,574,720 US$. After re-evaluation, the metal value is 25,073,568 US$.

A preliminary metallurgical test was done on 311 kg composite samples (28).

The average gold grade is 1.89 grams per tonnes Au.

The primery element is gold and other revenue genera-ting elements are copper, silver and sulfur with an average of 1.50%. The total recovery rate is 92%.

The metal value represent a share value of 1.52 US$ or 2.04 C$.

As new exploration results will be given in the second quarter of 2019, this will bring a different share value. To work towards a Pre-Feasability and Feasibility Study, Maple Gold mines will need further fundings. This will dilute the shares further; something that will have its effect on the share value.

None the less, Maple Gold Mines is a healthy company that has no problems to make ends meet. A quick ratio of the companies latest annual report is 3.22. This enables the company to go on with further exploration and drilling to add more resources to the project.

Maple Gold Mines has no debt and its insiders are loyal and have not been selling shares recently.

My personal opinion is that Maple Gold Mines is a buy and hold company with a good and healthy growth expectation. The company has an experienced managment team that has everything to move this project forward and maybe even prepare it towards an aquisition by a major.

Advanced Gold Exploration Companies in the Abitibi Greenstone Belt

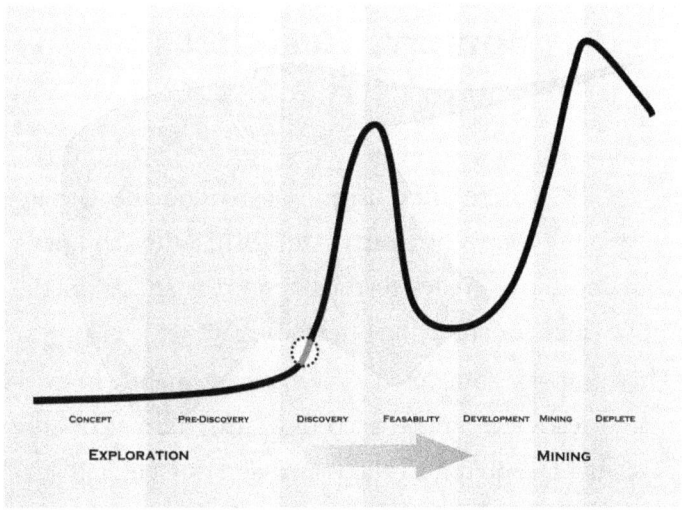

CONCEPT   PRE-DISCOVERY   DISCOVERY   FEASABILITY   DEVELOPMENT   MINING   DEPLETE

EXPLORATION   MINING

Bonterra Resources

Bonterra Resources is exploring the Urbanbarry property. In 2010, the company could ad more grades to their resources and is on the move since for something much bigger.

The company completed a merger agreement with Metanor resources and—according the terms of the agreement - aquired all the issued and outstanding shares of Metanor (29). Following the aquisition, Metanor shareholders are holding a balance of 42% of the company.

Bonterra and Metanor combined have High grade gold in the Gladiator and the Moroy deposits. Within the urban Barry Gold camp, the company has a significant upside potential in resources by doing further exploration. For the Moroy Deposit, the company has planned an updated NI 43-101 in 2019.

The Gladiator Deposit

The Gladiator deposit shows for now, only a mineral resource estimate of a technical report filed in 2012. This report mentions inferred resources of 905,000 tonnes with a 9.37 grams per tonnes Au grade. The metal value of these inferred resources are 345.91 US$ per tonnes, or a total metal value of 313,048,550 US$. After re-evaluation, the metal value is 203,481,557.5 US$.

Preliminary metallurgical studies mention a total gold recovery of at least 95% (30).

The fully permitted Gladiator project has an easy acces via provincial highway 113 that connects Chibougamau with Val d'Or. Power grid and other utilities are available in the workers camp (30).

Bonterra Resources also has an operational mill and has plans to expand the mill to a 2400 tonnes per day capacity somewhere mid 2019 (31).

According the latest and unaudited financial results ending februari 28, 2019 and 2018 (32), the company has a Quick Ratio of 1.57 and it seems to have no problems to pay the bills in 2019. The company has a low debt level and on top of that, it has 1.2 Million cash at hand. Insiders have only bought shares and did not sell any since mid 2018.

A management change of earlier this year created a price drop of its shares. The companies CEO Nav Dhaliwal and the companies' Vice President of exploration Dale Ginn have resigned there positions as directors (33). The newly announced management members are Mr Matthew Happyjack and Mr Akiba Leisman (34). The future will tell us if management has not lost its luster.

According the metal value and the financial results, the companies sharevalue is undervalued and should be around 3.75 US$ or 5,03 C$.

New estimated resources will increase the companies shareprice.

When Bonterra Resources is heading towards the Pre-Feasability Study, the company is in need of new fundings. The dilution of shares is normal for a exploration company in this stage of progress.

My personal opinion for Bonterra Resources is that it is a buy and hold company with a significant upwards cycle.

Advanced Gold Exploration Companies in the Abitibi Greenstone Belt

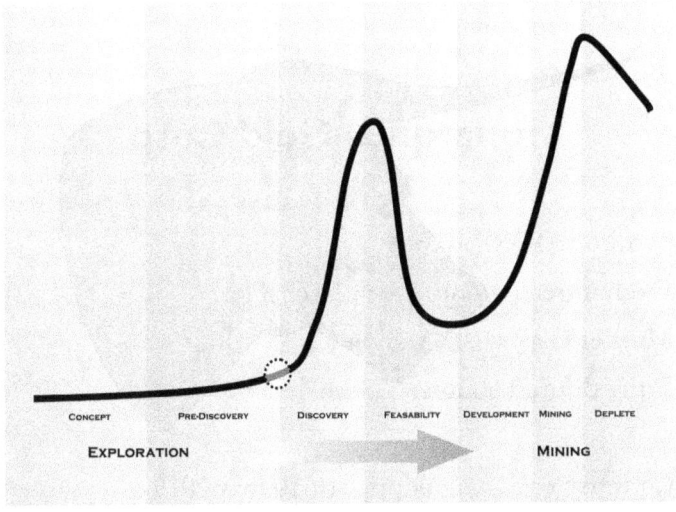

Quick Overview:

Monarques Gold Corp.

Symbol: MQR

Exchange: Toronto Stock Exchange

Market Cap: 60.06 Million C$

Fully diluted shares: 273 Million

Currency rate and goldprice of 10 may 2019

Share price: C$ 0.22

Gold price: 1286 US$

Exploration and developing:

Wasamac project

♦   **Inferred resources**: 4.16 Million tonnes
♦   Total metal value after re-calculation: 221,863,200 US$
♦   **Indicated resources**: 25.87 Million tonnes
♦   Total metal value after re-evaluation:

2,099,402,240 US$

♦ **Measured resources:** 3.99 Million tonnes

♦ Total metal value after re-evaluation: 299,984,160 US$

♦ **Proven resources:** 1.028 Million tonnes

♦ Total metal value: 101,977,600 US$

♦ **Probable resources:** 20.4 Million tonnes

♦ Total metal value: 1,950,165,690 US$

The **total metal value** of the Wasamac project is 4,673,392,890 US$.

Croinor Gold project

♦ **Measured resources:** 251,000 tonnes

♦ Total metal value after re-evaluation: 53,313,861.31 US$

♦ **Indicated resources:** 2.26 Million tonnes

♦ Total metal value after re-evaluation: 600,391,956 US$

♦ **Inferred resources:** 425,610 tonnes

♦ Total metal value after re-evaluation: 66,621,565.73 US$

The **total metal value** of the Croinor Gold project is 720,327,383.04 US$.

McKenzie Break project

Total metal value of scenario 1 is 142,465,346.38 US$

Total metal value of scenario 2 is 122,975,769.86 US$

Swanson project

- **Indicated resources:** 1,752,100 tonnes
- Total metal value after re-evaluation: 96,469,441.6 US$
- **Inferred resources:** 74,000 tonnes
- Total metal value after re-evaluation: 5,320,390.4 US$

The **total metal value** of the Swanson project is 101,789,832 US$.

The Beaufor mine

- **Proven resources:** 28,100 tonnes
- Total metal value: 6,235,390 US$
- **Probable resources:** 111,500 tonnes
- Total metal value: 29,315,580 US$
- **Measured resources:** 74,400 tonnes
- Total metal value after re-evaluation: 14,894,284.8 US$
- **Indicated resources:** 271,700 tonnes
- Total metal value after re-evaluation: 64,282,046.4 US$
- **Inferred resources:** 46,100 tonnes
- Total metal value after re-evaluation: 9,320,013.95 US$

The **total metal value** of the Beaufor mine is 124,047,315.15 US$

The Simkar Gold project

- **Measured resources:** 33,570 tonnes
- Total metal value after re-evaluation: 4,717,256.4 US$
- **Indicated resources:** 208,470 tonnes
- Total metal value after re-evaluation: 35,203,078.08 US$
- **Inferred resources:** 98,320 tonnes
- Total metal value after re-evaluation: 15,158,338.52 US$

The **total metal value** of the Simkar Gold project is 55,078,673 US$.

Probe Metals Inc

Symbol: PRB

Exchange: Canadian Venture Exchange

Market Cap: 124 Million C$

Fully diluted shares: 127.7 Million

Currency rate and goldprice of 18 may 2019

Share price: C$ 0.97

Gold price: 1278 US$

Exploration

The Beliveau Deposit

- **Indicated resources:** 7,510,700 tonnes
- Total metal value after re-evaluation: 552,246,749.6 US$
- **Inferred resources:** 6,215,700 tonnes
- Total metal value after re-evaluation: 398,283,408.9 US$

The total metal value of the Beliveau deposit is 950,530,158.5 US$.

The North Deposit

♦ **Indicated resources:** 837,700 tonnes

♦ Total metal value after re-evaluation: 38,252,732.8 US$

♦ **Inferred resources:** 1,820,000 tonnes

♦ Total metal value after re-evaluation: 74,091,290 US$

The total value of the North Deposit is 112,344,022.8 US$.

The Highway Deposit

♦ **Indicated resources:** 687,800 tonnes

♦ Total metal value after re-evaluation: 37,724,454.4 US$

♦ **Inferred resources:** 748,800 tonnes

♦ Total metal value after re-evaluation: 31,568,659.2 US$

Total metal value of the Highway Deposit is
69,293,113.6 US$.

The South Deposit

- **Inferred resources:** 519,400 tonnes
- Total metal value after re-evaluation:
37,160,732.7 US$

Radisson Mining Resources

Symbol: RDS

Exchange: Toronto Stock Exchange Venture Exchange

Market Cap: 17.8 Million C$

Fully diluted shares: 148,367,360 Class A shares

Currency rate and goldprice of 19 may 2019

Share price: C$ 0.12

Gold price: 1278 US$

Exploration

The O'Brien deposit

♦   **Indictated resources:** 1,125,447 tonnes

♦   Total metal value after re-evaluation: 215,230,484.28 US$

♦   **Inferred resopurces:** 1,157,021 tonnes

♦   Total metal value after re-evaluation: 70,287,868.73 US$

The total metal value of the O'Brien deposit is 285,518,353.01 US$.

Maple Gold Mines

Symbol: MGM

Exchange: Canadian Venture Exchange

Market Cap: 24.2 Million C$

Fully diluted shares: 302,652,306

Currency rate and goldprice of 20 may 2019

Share price: C$ 0.08

Gold price: 1276 US$

Exploration

Douay West Zone

- **Indicated resources:** 3,693,000 tonnes
- Total metal value after re-evaluation: 270,032,160 US$
- **Inferred resources:** 2,932,000 tonnes
- Total metal value after re-evaluation: 98,034,352 US$.

The **total metal value** of the Douay West Zone deposit is: 368,066,512 US$.

531 Zone

- Inferred resources: 4,998,000 tonnes
- Total metal value after re-evaluation: 159,901,014 US$

Maine Zone

- Inferred resources: 1,849,000 tonnes
- Total metal value after re-evaluation: 63,601,902 US$

Zone 10

- Inferred resources: 1,864,000 tonnes
- Total metal value after re-evaluation: 51,105,288 US$

North West Zone

- Inferred resources: 828,000 tonnes
- Total metal value after re-evaluation: 35,849,502 US$

Zone 20

- Inferred resources: 1,685,000 tonnes
- Total metal value after re-evaluation: 27,961,732 US$

Central Zone

- Inferred resources: 1,086,000 tonnes
- Total metal value after re-evaluation: 25,073,568 US$

Bonterra resources

Symbol: BTR

Exchange: Toronto Stock Exchange Venture Exchange

Market Cap: C$ 94.5 Million

Fully diluted shares: 54.3 Million

Currency rate and goldprice of 21 may 2019

Share price: C$ 1.74

Gold price: 1273 US$

Exploration

The Gladiator deposit

- Inferred resources: 905,000 tonnes
- Total metal value after re-evaluation: 203,481,557.5 US$

Update of
Potentials: War for nuclear facilities or war for oil?

In "**Potentials: War for nuclear facilities or war for oil?**", I introduced you to three companies that had a significant upcycle in there stockprice since the publication of the book. Tip advisors or other newsletter writers have a tendency to show off with results that they have gained. Unfortunatly, they only show gains and never their losses which are also significant. If not, they would not be afraid to talk about these stocks.

The Potentials series do not only offer you a deep insight, but they enable you to follow every single stock the author is talking about, the winners ànd the losers.

In "Potentials: War for nuclear facilities or war for oil?" I shortly brieved of 3 companies, Kratos Defence & Security Solutions Inc, Shoal Point Energy and Union Jack Oil (35).

Please be awere that the update is done on 28 may 2019 and that update numbers are based on this date.

The investors, who became owner of Kratos Defence & Security Solutions in October 2018 at the price of 12.58 US$, gained a nice upgrade in sharevalue of 70%.

This means that gains where made at 10% each month on the base price of 12.58 US$ (no compound). For those who read the book, you will remember that most likely, the fun ain't over yet.

For Shoal Point Energy, those that own the stock since October 28th on a stockprice of 0.03 C$, the stock soared by more than 100% by March 21st 2019 to as high as 0.08 C$ (150% to be precise).

This was much earlier as expected because of the oil price increase due geopolitical issues early 2019. After oil prices dropped again, the stock went down with it.

As we look at the geopolitical tensions between Iran and the USA, and nevertheless the situation in Venezuela, Shoal Point Energy has all in house to play the same game again. I expect the stocks to soar again in a few months from now. All depends on the situation with Iran.

My expectation is that the stockpiling of oil by the USA, which tends to bring down the oilprice a little, will explode when Iran will block the Persian Gulf and the Street of Hormous. Many countries wil have problems to get enough oil, somekind of a rerun if you will of what happened in the 1970's.

The USA will sell their stocks at exploded prices, which will probably skyrocket the petrol price at the gasoline stations once again.

And last but not least, I brought up a Brittish Oil exploration company, Union Jack Oil PLC.

Those who have bought shares on date of November 3th at a stockprice of 0.10 Brittish Pound, when a short analysis for the potential was done, is now enjoying a comfortable gain of 40%.

Afterword

In this Potentials, the author has selected 5 gold exploration companies that could have—according to his opinion—a significant upward cycle in growth.

The resources mentioned for each deposit do not guarantee however that a certain stock will forfill its expectations, all depends on what the market will decide and as you know, the market is always right.

The author showed companies with their deposits but that does not mean that all deposits are real reserves and not all deposits have enough reserves to be mined due to the all-in sustaining costs. All opinions are these of the author, and of the author alone. They can not be seen as investing advice and you always have to do your own due dilligence before investing.

All companies that are spoken of in this Potentials are subject to further updates that will be made public on a regular base in the Potentials book series.

And please remember:

NEVER INVEST IN COMMODITIES WHAT YOU CANNOT AFFORD TO LOOSE.

Sources:

1. monarquesgold.com
2. monarquesgold.com/en/our-assets/val-d-or/wasamac
3. monarquesgoldfiles.com/documents/files/Corporate-Presentation-PDF-EN.pdf
4. monarquesgoldfiles.com/documents/files/Corporate-Presentation-PDF-EN.pdf
5. monarquesgoldfiles.com/documents/files/43-101/Wasamac-feasibility-study.pdf
6. monarquesgoldfiles.com/documents/files/43-101/43-101-Croinor-Gold.pdf
7. monarquesgold.com/en/our-assets/val-d-or/mckenzie-break
8. monarquesgold.com/en/our-assets/val-d-or/swanson
9. monarquesgoldfiles.com/documents/files/43-101/NI-43-101-Swanson-Property.pdf
10. monarquesgold.com/en/our-assets/val-d-or/beaufor-mine
11. monarquesgold.com/en/our-assets/val-d-or/camflo-mill
12. monarquesgold.com/en/our-assets/val-d-or/beacon-mill
13. monarquesgoldfiles.com/documents/files/2018/Monarques-FS-Q2-2018-12-31-EN.pdf
14. monarquesgold.com/en/our-assets/val-d-or/simkar-gold

15. The Northern Miner: December 6, 2016 Volume 102 Number 46 December 26, 2016 – January 1, 2017

16. The Northern Miner: January 18, 2017 Volume 103 Number 5 March 6 – 19, 2017

17. The Northern Miner: February 21, 2018 Volume 104 Number 5 March 5 – 18, 2018

18. probemetals.com/site/assets/files/1191/2019_05_07_probe_metals_presentation.pdf

19. northernminer.com/news/radisson-mining-withdraws-from-eastmain-mine/1000097958/

20. northernminer.com/news/radisson-mining-withdraws-15-5-million-prospectus/1000099164/

21. The Northern Miner: June 27, 2011 Volume 97 Number 19 Jun 27 - Jul 3, 2011

22. radissonmining.com/wp-content/uploads/43_101_obrien_-2018-1.pdf

23. maplegoldmines.com/index.php/en/projects/douay-gold-project/92-exploration-history

24. Northern Miner: May 24, 2018 Volume 104 Number 12 June 11 – June 24, 2018

25. google.com/search?client=firefox-b-d&q=maple+gold+mines+stock+price

26. maplegoldmines.com/images/pdf/2019/corporate_presentation/April_2019_-_MGM_Investor_Slide_Deck.pdf

Potentials: investing opportunities for everyone, no matter the size of your wallet.

27. maplegoldmines.com/images/pdf/2018/
Douay_NI_43_101_Technical_Report_March_2018.pdf

28. maplegoldmines.com/index.php/en/projects/preliminary-metallurgy

29. Northern Miner: September 27, 2018 Volume 104 Number 19 October 1 – 14, 2018

30. btrgold.com/2019/05/01/bonterra-provides-corporate-update/

31. btrgold.com/2019/05/01/bonterra-provides-corporate-update/

32. btrgold.com/wp-content/uploads/2019/05/2019-Q3.pdf

33. Northern Miner: February 12, 2019 Volume 105 Number 4 February 18 – March 3, 2019

34. btrgold.com/2019/03/26/bonterra-appoints-matthew-happyjack-as-director/

35. www.amazon.co.uk/War-nuclear-facilities-war-opportunities/dp/1729667821/ref=sr_1_4?
keywords=war+for+nuclear+facilities&qid=1559052784&s=gateway&sr=8-4

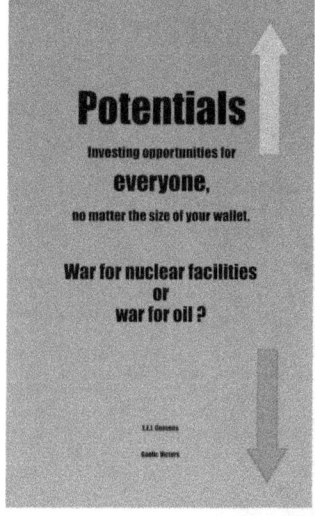